THE

ADVANTAGE OF MISFORTUNE:

A

P O E M.

" Whatever is, is right."

L O N D O N:

Printed for J. RIDLEY, in St. James's Street.

MDCCLXXIII.

[Price One Shilling.]

TO

EDWARD JERNINGHAM, ESQ.

THIS POEM

IS INSCRIBED

BY HIS OBEDIENT HUMBLE SERVANT,

THE AUTHOR.

THE

ADVANTAGE of MISFORTUNE:

A

P   O   E   M.

BY nations fear'd, refpected, and obey'd,
Bozaldab long had Egypt's fceptre fway'd.
Great was his pow'r, extenfive his domain,
Unnumber'd bleffings crown'd his happy reign;
For him the Earth unlock'd her richeft ftores,   5
And wealth to Egypt flow'd from diftant fhores.
Thus great, thus honour'd, thus fupremely bleft;
No wifh remain'd beyond what he poffeft.
Alas! while pleafure fill'd the fmiling fcene,
He little thought a change fhould intervene,   10

B   But,

But, judging ftill the future by the paft,
Believ'd the momentary blifs fhould laft.
Attendant on his ftate the fervile train
By flatt'ry fought their Monarch's love to gain;
Till fwell'd with pride, with dignity elate,   15
He deem'd himfelf beyond the reach of Fate.
Unhappy wretch! condemn'd ere long to prove
The juft refentment of the Pow'rs above;
To know, that man was deftin'd ftill to bear,
And life a fcene of vanity and care;   20
To feel, that Grandeur's but an empty name,
And only Virtue merits lafting fame.
His only Son, the darling of his age,
One that might well a Parent's love engage;
For whom he toil'd by day, and watch'd by night, 25
Joy of his foul, and fource of his delight;
Meets in the chace an arrow wing'd with death,
And in his Father's arms refigns his breath.
Struck dumb with horror, frantic with defpair,
BOZALDAB fmote his breaft, and tore his hair.   30
To footh his anguifh in this dreadful hour,
His numerous train exert their little pow'r:

To

[3]

To them, in accents terrible and wild,
He anfwer'd, gazing on his breathlefs Child,

  " Hence, idle flatterers! that vainly call   35
" Bozaldab Lord and Monarch over all;
" Who fay that life depends upon his breath,
" And call his frown more terrible than death.
" Behold the object of my tend'reft cares,
" The promis'd comfort of declining years!   40
" Say, can this boafted pow'r my Child reftore?
" Then talk of Empire, and of Crowns, no more.
" Thus fnatch'd away, ere half his courfe was run,
" Unhappy hour!—alas, my Son! my Son!"

  The Monarch ceas'd, and proftrate on the ground, 45
Embrac'd his child, and kift the ghaftly wound;
Then ftarting up, diftraction in his look,
The trembling train with eager hafte forfook,
And to the gloomy grotto bent his way,
Where roll'd in duft, oppreft with grief he lay.   50
Night now approach'd; no noife was heard around,
Save the fad fcreech-owl's melancholy found:

                But

[4]

But peace, nor reſt, the wretched Parent knew;
His tears the boſom of the earth bedew;
Unable longer to contain his grief, 55
He ſought, in vain complaints, to find relief.

" Periſh!" he cried, " the pow'r that could not ſave
" My only Son, my darling, from the grave.
" Was it for this, thro' many tedious years
" I brav'd ſuch dangers? bore ſuch toils and cares? 60
" Was it for this I labour'd to extend
" An Empire that ſhall ne'er to him deſcend?
" And can that God be merciful and juſt,
" Who lays our fondeſt wiſhes in the duſt?
" A Being really good, and truly wiſe, 65
" Beholds his creatures with paternal eyes;
" Nor thus delights with tears their cup to fill,
" To pleaſe his humour, his capricious will.
" This wretched life I can no longer bear:
" Welcome, oh Death! thou kind releaſe from care!"

He ſpoke—and rais'd the dagger to his breaſt,
When, lo, to view an Angel ſtood confeſt!

Thick

Thick flafh'd the light'ning, loud the thunder roar'd ;
BOZALDAB faw, fell proftrate, and ador'd.
" Rife," faid the Angel, " fear not, but obey ; 75
" Intrepid follow where I lead the way."
Together they afcend the mountain's brow,
Whofe height commands the vaft expanfe below.
" Turn hence thine eyes, exclaim'd the heav'nly guide;
" No longer doubt, be humble, and confide." 80

BOZALDAB now perceiv'd a defert ifle,
Where niggard Nature never deign'd to fmile.
On this inhofpitable fhore was caft
A wretch, whofe ev'ry breath ftill feem'd the laft:
Pale Famine in his meagre look appear'd ; 85
To Heav'n in fpeechlefs agony he rear'd
His trembling hands,—and begg'd fome fmall relief,
Some little comfort in this hour of grief.
The diftant howl of beafts affright his ear ;
Each moment brings the dreaded danger near. 90
A cafket, held within his feeble hand,
He now indignant caft upon the fand.
" Ye glitt'ring gems," he cried, " fo lately priz'd,
" Well do ye merit to be thus defpis'd ;

C   " Deceitful

" Deceitful riches !—your delufive pow'r   95
" Has wrought the dreadful mis'ry of this hour.
" Now, now, I feel the bitternefs of want,
" And need that pity I refus'd to grant.
" Alas ! had my inhofpitable door,
" When Fortune fmil'd, been open to the poor; 100
" Had I to Sorrow lent a pitying ear,
" Heav'n would not thus rejeᚏ my ardent pray'r."

He ceas'd, and once more rais'd his dying eyes
O'er the vaſt Ocean, and from far defcries
A veſſel fwift advancing to the view,   105
And near the barren ſhore ere long it drew.
A ray of hope now darted on his mind ;
" From men," he cried, " I fure ſhall pity find :"
Then to the crew he offers half his ſtore,
If they would land him on fome happier ſhore.   110
They hear relentlefs, but with greedy eyes
Behold, and eager view the glitt'ring prize :
At length, by fordid avarice impell'd,
They feize the part the trembling wretch with-held :
Reproaches, tears, were all employ'd in vain ; 115
Regardlefs of his pray'rs, the ſhip they gain.
                              " Inhabitant

" Inhabitant of Heav'n !" Bozaldab cries,
" Canſt thou behold, with calm, with tranquil eyes,
" Crimes thus unpuniſh'd ? mis'ry thus oppreſt?
" Has Heav'n no pity then for man diſtreſt ?" 120

To him replied the Miniſter of Peace,
" Let all thy doubts, unhappy murm'rer, ceaſe.
" Miſtaken Monarch ! ignorant and vain,
" No more the ways of Providence arraign.
" Behold that ſhip, ſhort-ſighted as thou art, 125
" In which the wretched Merchant wiſh'd to part ;
" See it the ſport of waves, by tempeſts toſt,
" Daſh'd on that rock, and in a moment loſt !
" Doſt thou not hear the ſinking ſailors' cries ?
" Tho' thou art blind, acknowledge God is wiſe. 130
" Preſume no more thy Maker to direct ;
" Adore his juſtice, his decrees reſpect.
" The man thy pity wiſhes to relieve,
" When Heav'n ſees fit, ſhall ſuccour ſtill receive ;
" Taught by this uſeful leſſon, he ſhall know 135
" To feel compaſſion for another's woe ;
       " Misfortune

" Misfortune fhall inlarge his narrow heart,
" No longer fhall he fear with wealth to part;
" By fordid avarice no more mifled,
" By him the poor be cloath'd, the hungry fed. 140
" Another fcene attention now commands,
" An object dearer far thine eye demands."

BOZALDAB look'd, and to his ravifh'd eyes
Inftant a ftately Palace feem'd to rife :
The walls were polifh'd ivory and gold, 145
Enrich'd with gems, refplendent to behold;
Adorn'd with ftatues of his noble line,
Of jafper form'd, and wrought with fkill divine.
Here on a throne, by proftrate flaves ador'd,
BOZALDAB faw his Son, fo much deplor'd; 150
The loft ABORAM—feated by his fide,
In fplendid majefty, his blooming Bride.

" It is, it is my fon !" BOZALDAB cried,
" No longer to his wretched Sire denied;
" Oh let me once more clafp him to my heart! 155
" My lov'd ABORAM, we will never part!"

" Reftrain

" Reſtrain thyſelf," the beauteous Angel ſaid,
" Thou canſt not graſp an unſubſtantial ſhade.
" Thou ſee'ſt, had Heav'n allow'd a longer date,
" What would have been thy lov'd Aboram's fate."

" And why," the Monarch eagerly replies,
" Why was this bliſs refus'd a Parent's eyes ?"
" Once more obſerve," rejoin'd the heavenly guide,
" View the laſt ſcene, and let thy heart decide."

But ſcarce Bozaldab could the picture know: 165
That face, where vivid health was wont to glow,
Deform'd with paſſion, dreadfully expreſt
The rage, the fury, lurking in his breaſt.
Of what he was, no likeneſs now remain'd ;
His frame convuls'd—his hands with blood were ſtain'd.
The ſplendid palace levell'd with the ground,
Aboram ſeiz'd, and in a dungeon bound ;
On the cold ground depriv'd of ſight he lay,
For ever barr'd the chearful light of day :
His ſlaves, the abject creatures of his pow'r,   175
Inſult his mis'ry in this dreadful hour ;

D   And

And fhe, who fhould in ev'ry grief have fhar'd,
Now for her Lord the poifon'd bowl prepar'd.
He takes the fatal draught,—the fcene was o'er,
'Twas finifh'd now—and ABORAM no more.　　180

" Eternal Wifdom! humbly thus I bow,"
BozALDAB cried, " I feel thy goodnefs now:
" Thou didft exert thy pow'r, my Child to fave
" From guilt, from mis'ry, by an early grave;
" Crown'd him on earth with never-dying fame, 185
" Preferv'd, immortaliz'd, his much-lov'd name.
" I own my error, humbled in the duft;
" Thy works are good, and all thy ways are juft."

" Thrice happy he," th' angelic form replies,
" Whofe erring mind Affliction renders wife. 190
" Now caft the fatal dagger from thy breaft,
" And own, what Heav'n ordains is ever beft;
" Hereafter by this ufeful leffon learn,
" Man fees in part, nor can the whole difcern.
" And fhall he then, felf-confident and vain, 195
" Prefume his great Creator to arraign?

　　　　　　　　　　　　" Say,

" Say, can the reaſon, that to man is lent,
" Of perfect knowledge meaſure the extent?
" In Him who clearly ſees, then place thy truſt;
" Doubt not, though thou art frail, that God is juſt.
" On Him rely—complain, repine no more,
" Enough for thee to tremble and adore."

The Angel ſpoke, and inſtant wing'd his flight
To the pure regions of eternal light.

The E N D.